50 STATES

Celebrating
TEXAS

WITHDRAWN

The text of this book is set in Weidemann.
The display type is set in Bernard Gothic.
The illustrations are drawn with pencil and colored digitally.
The maps are pen, ink, and watercolor.

Photograph of armadillo on page 32 © 2013 sdbower/Fotolia
Photograph of Texas longhorn on page 32 © 2013 Corbis
Photograph of bat on page 32 © 2013 Corbis
Photograph of mockingbird on page 32 © 2013 imagebroker.net/Superstock
Photograph of golden bluebonnet on page 32 © 2013 Radius Images/Alamy

Library of Congress Cataloging-in-Publication Data:
Bauer, Marion Dane.
Celebrating Texas : 50 states to celebrate / by Marion Dane Bauer ;
illustrated by C. B. Canga.
p. cm. — (50 states to celebrate) (Green light readers level 3)
ISBN 978-0-547-98395-0 (paper over board) — ISBN 978-0-547-89786-8 (trade paper)
1. Texas—Juvenile literature. I. Canga, C. B., ill. II. Title.
F386.3.B38 2013
976.4—dc23
2012016881

Manufactured in China
SCP 10 9 8 7 6 5 4 3 2 1
4500400243

50 STATES TO CELEBRATE

Celebrating
TEXAS

Written by **Marion Dane Bauer**
Illustrated by **C. B. Canga**

sandpiper

Houghton Mifflin Harcourt

Boston   New York   2013

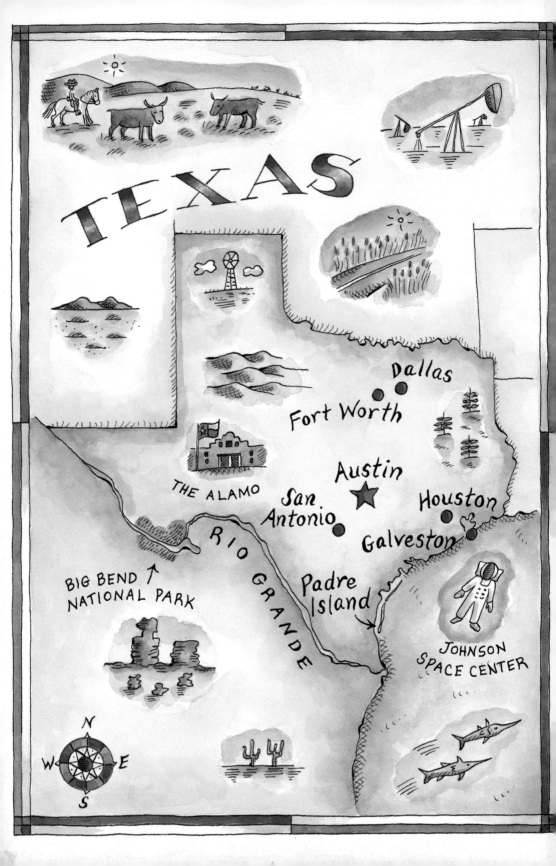

Hi! I'm Mr. Geo.
Welcome to the second
biggest state in the United States.
The Lone Star State.
Texas, of course!

Texas was our biggest state until Alaska
became a state in 1959.

1

Can you find Texas on the map?
It borders another country and four states.
Look between Mexico and Oklahoma.

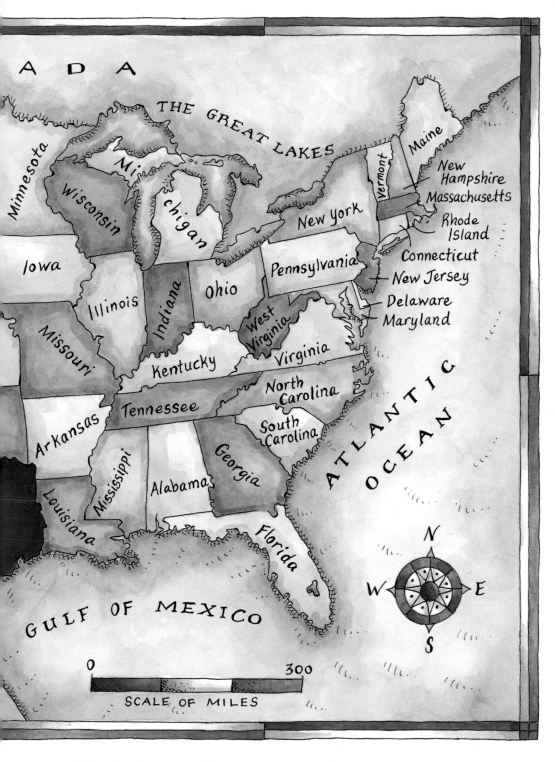

Now look west of Louisiana and Arkansas,
and east of New Mexico.
That big place you see is Texas!

Texas is famous for its **rodeos**.
Here I am at the Houston
Livestock Show and Rodeo.
It's one of the biggest rodeos in the country.
I'm looking forward to a
wild ride on this **bronco**!

Cowboys from Mexico taught American
settlers how to ride, rope, and **herd**.

The first Texas rodeo took place in 1883.
Cowboys held a contest to see who could rope
and tie a **steer** the fastest.
Look out for those **longhorns**!

Did you know?

Cowhands herd cattle through the
streets of Fort Worth's historic section
twice a day for visitors to see.

Texas is known for big, modern cities, too.

Look! Glassy skyscrapers in Dallas.

A high-tech space center in Houston.

An elegant statehouse in Austin.

A busy port in Galveston.

Lots of shops and restaurants in San Antonio.

It's a good thing my boots are made for riding *and* walking!

Touring around Texas makes me hungry.
There are so many different foods to try here.
Have you ever tasted chicken-fried steak?
Yum!
Or **enchiladas** and **tamales**?
Delicious!

Of course, Texas is famous for its chili.

Hot and spicy!

But what I love best is a good old Texas barbecue.

Pass the ribs and cornbread this way, please!

Now that my belly is full, I'm ready to dance!
That country and western band sounds great.

Let's try the Texas two-step first.

Fast, fast, slow. Fast, fast, slow.

If only my feet could keep up with the music!

How about line dancing?

Everyone can join in!

Texas is changeable.

The weather changes from season to season.

The landscape changes from place to place.

I found these **armadillos** on the **prairie**.

Wild hogs scared me in the forest.

At the coast, I love watching pelicans
scoop up fish into their big bills.

I spotted a cougar high in the mountains once.
And it's a good thing I saw that rattlesnake
in the desert before he saw me!

The first people in Texas were Native Americans. They lived here for thousands of years before explorers from other places came.

In fact, the name Texas comes from a **Caddo** word pronounced *TAY-shas.*

It means "friends."

The Caddo are Native Americans who farmed land in eastern Texas.
They lived in forests of tall pine trees.
They built homes with thick grass and shaped them like beehives.

The first Europeans to come here were explorers from Spain.
I like visiting the many **missions** they built.
The Alamo is the most famous of them all.

People say "Remember the Alamo" because many Texans died there during a heroic battle in 1836.

Today, people from many **cultures** live in Texas.

Sometimes they have special celebrations.

Parades! Picnics! Block parties!

Costumes! Concerts! Fireworks!

I love being a part of it all.

Cinco de Mayo, on May 5, celebrates Mexican heritage. Juneteenth, on June 19, honors the end of slavery in the United States.

Two big cities are named after Texas heroes.
Austin is the state capital.
It's named after Stephen F. Austin,
who's called the Father of Texas.
He helped 300 families start new lives
on the Texas **frontier** in the 1820s.

The city of Houston was named after Sam Houston.
He led Texas to freedom from Mexico during the
Texas Revolution.
When Texas was its own country, he was
president twice.

SAM HOUSTON

STEPHEN AUSTIN

Have you ever heard of black gold?
That's what they called oil in Texas
when it was first discovered here in 1901.
Mud, gas, and oil shot nearly 100 feet into the air
at a well called Spindletop.
Soon, oil was as valuable as gold!

Spindletop was not the first oil well in Texas, but it was the beginning of the oil boom.
People rushed to Texas looking for oil and jobs.
New businesses sprang up all over the state.

Did you know?

Oil is used to make gasoline and other fuels. Texas produces more oil than any other state in the United States.

Texas is rich in more than oil.
It is rich in farms and ranches, too.
One ranch, the King Ranch, has
825,000 acres of land.
That's almost as big as the state of Rhode Island.
Lots of horses and cattle live there.

Texas farms grow many crops.

Cotton is a leading crop.

My favorite, though, is pecans.

Would you like a taste of my pecan pie?

Did you know?
Texas also grows lots of grapefruits.

Texans sure do love their sports.
Especially football!
They have two professional football teams,
the Houston Texans and the Dallas Cowboys.

The Cowboys won five of the eight
Super Bowl games they played.

The Texas Rangers and the Houston Astros play baseball for Texas.
The Houston Rockets, the Dallas Mavericks, and the San Antonio Spurs give fans a lot to cheer about during basketball season.

All around Texas, there are
many places to explore.
Fair Park in Dallas has museums, monuments,
shows, and parks to enjoy all year long.
At Padre Island, I like to gather seashells and
splash in the waves.

And it's always fun to hunt for **fossils**
at Big Bend National Park.
Maybe this fossil is from a flying dinosaur!

Have you ever wondered what it feels like
to blast off into space?
You can find out at the Johnson Space Center
in Houston.
You can tour the places where astronauts train.
Look! We can see right into Mission Control!

The first word ever broadcasted from the moon
was "Houston." Neil Armstrong said, "Houston,
Tranquility Base here. The *Eagle* has landed."

The River Walk in San Antonio is one of the most
pleasant places I know.
Rippling water.
Towering cypress trees.
Places to eat, shop, wander, and watch
the crowds go by.

The River Walk is about 13 miles long
and includes many different parts.

Always, though, when I visit Texas, I look
forward to the rodeo.
Riding, racing, and roping!
Cowhands, cattle, and clowns!
Food, fun, and fiddle music!

It all makes me feel like I'm in the Old West . . .
even if I never get the hang of staying on this
bucking bronco!

Fast Facts About Texas

Nickname: The Lone Star State, because of the lone star on the state flag from the time Texas was a separate country.

State motto: Friendship.

State capital: Austin.

Other major cities: Beaumont, Dallas, El Paso, Corpus Christi, Galveston, Fort Worth, Houston, San Antonio.

Year of statehood: 1845.

State animal: Small animal, armadillo. Large animal, Texas longhorn. Flying mammal, bat.

State bird: Mockingbird.

State flower: Bluebonnet.

State flag

Population: Just over 25 million people, according to the 2010 census.

Fun fact: Four presidents of the United States lived in Texas for some part of their lives: Dwight D. Eisenhower, Lyndon B. Johnson, George H. W. Bush, and his son George W. Bush.

Dates in Texas History

1519: The coastline of Texas is mapped by Alonso Alvarez de Pineda from Spain.

1528: After a shipwreck, Spanish explorers arrive in Texas for the first time.

1540: The Spanish explorer Francisco Vásquez de Coronado travels across west Texas.

1821: Mexico wins independence from Spain; Texas becomes a part of Mexico.

1822: Stephen F. Austin helps 300 families settle on the frontier.

1830: Mexico forbids U.S. colonists from establishing more settlements in Texas; it also bans slaves from being brought to the area.

1835: The Texas Revolution begins.

1836: Texas wins **independence** from Mexico. It becomes its own country called the **Republic of Texas**.

1845: Texas joins the United States as the 28th state.

1861: Texas **secedes** from the United States and joins the **Confederate States of America** during the **Civil War**.

1865: Civil War ends; Texas soon rejoins the United States.

1865: Cattle drives begin, with cowboys moving herds as large as 3,000 along Texas trails to Kansas.

1901: Oil is discovered at a hill called Spindletop near Beaumont, Texas.

1963: NASA opens a space center in Houston.

1996: The Dallas Cowboys win their fifth Super Bowl Championship.

2008: Hurricane Ike strikes the Galveston/Houston area.

Activities

1. **LOCATE** the four states that border Texas on the map on pages 2 and 3. Then SAY each state's name out loud.

2. **DESIGN** a magazine page about exciting things to see and do in Texas. Include words and picture in your magazine page.

3. **SHARE** two facts you learned about Texas with a family member or friend.

4. **PRETEND** you live in Texas and you have relatives from another state visiting for the first time. Your cousins have lots of questions about Texas. See if you can correctly answer them.

   a. In **WHAT** Texas city is a high-tech space center located? (Hint: It's called the Johnson Space Center)

   b. **WHEN** did the heroic battle at the Alamo take place?

   c. **WHO** brought 300 families to the Texas frontier in the 1820s?

   d. **HOW** did the state of Texas get its name?

5. **UNJUMBLE** these words that have something to do with Texas. Write your answers on a separate sheet of paper.

   a. **DROOE** (HINT: A place where cowboys and cowgirls show their skills to an audience.)

   b. **BCEBAREU** (HINT: A kind of food people enjoy in Texas)

   c. **DIAMRLLOA** (HINT: A Texas prairie animal)

   d. **MLAAO** (HINT: A famous battle site)

   e. **CTOTNO** (HINT: A Texas crop)

Glossary

armadillo: a burrowing animal whose body is covered with bony plates. (p. 12)

bronco: a horse that has not been trained for riding. (p. 4)

bucking: leaping upward with head down in a wild way. (p. 31)

Caddo: Native American people who lived in east Texas before Spanish explorers arrived. (p. 14)

Civil War: the war between the Northern states and the Southern states that ended slavery in the United States. (p. 33)

Confederate States of America: the group of 11 Southern states that separated from the United States from 1861–65 and fought in the Civil War against the United States. (p. 33)

culture: the customs, beliefs, and ways of living shared by a group of people. (p. 17)

drought: a long period of time with little or no rain. (p. 12)

enchilada: a type of food that includes meat or cheese rolled in a tortilla and baked in chili sauce. This food has its origins in Mexican culture. (p. 8)

fossil: the remains of a prehistoric plant or animal that has become hardened or turned into rock. A fossil may be a skeleton, a shell, a footprint, or the imprint of a leaf. (p. 27)

frontier: a region that is just beyond or at the edge of a newly settled area. (p. 18)

herd: to move animals together. (p. 4)

independence: freedom from being ruled or governed by another country. (p. 33) longhorn: a breed of cattle with long horns that curve outward. (p. 5)

mission: a place where religious and cultural ideas can be taught. (p. 16)

prairie: a wide area of flat or rolling land with tall grass and few trees. (p. 12)

republic: a government in which people elect representatives to make the laws. (p. 33)

Republic of Texas: the name for Texas when it was a country of its own from 1836–45. (p. 33)

rodeo: a public show in which skills such as riding broncos and roping calves are displayed. (p. 4)

secede: to withdraw membership. (p. 33)

steer: a young male cattle, raised for beef. (p. 5)

tamale: a type of food made of fried chopped meat and crushed peppers wrapped in cornhusks and steamed; this food has its origins in Mexican culture. (p. 8)

Texas Revolution: the war Texas fought to gain freedom from Mexico and become its own country called the Republic of Texas. (p. 19)

Answers to activities on page 34:

1) Louisiana, Arkansas, Oklahoma, and New Mexico;
2) magazine pages will vary; 3) answers will vary; 4a) Houston, 4b) 1836, 4c) Stephen F. Austin, 4d) It comes from the Caddo or Native American word pronounced *TAY-shas* that means "friends," 5a) RODEO, 5b) BARBECUE, 5c) ARMADILLO, 5d) ALAMO, 5e) COTTON.